CHIMERA

poems by

Brad Buchanan

Finishing Line Press
Georgetown, Kentucky

CHIMERA

Copyright © 2022 by Brad Buchanan
ISBN 979-8-88838-039-0 First Edition
All rights reserved under International and Pan-American Copyright Conventions. No part of this book may be reproduced in any manner whatsoever without written permission from the publisher, except in the case of brief quotations embodied in critical articles and reviews.

ACKNOWLEDGMENTS

"Atrophy Wife" first appeared in *Sacramento Voices*.
"The Butterfly Effect" first appeared in appeared in *Equinox*.
"Cogito Roulette" first appeared in *The Esthetic Apostle*.
"Morning Glory" first appeared in *ELM*. It has also subsequently appeared in *The Stray Branch*.
"The Day I Took No Pain Medication" first appeared in Live Encounters.
"On 'Cheating Death'" first appeared in *Live Encounters*.
"Selling Home" first appeared in *The Fiddlehead*.
"Tempest" first appeared in *The New Orleans Review*.

I gratefully acknowledge Joshua Lurie-Terrell for providing the author photo and designing the cover art, and for giving his permission for their publication.

Publisher: Leah Huete de Maines
Editor: Christen Kincaid
Cover Art and Design: Joshua Lurie-Terrell
Author Photo: Joshua Lurie-Terrell

Order online: www.finishinglinepress.com
also available on amazon.com

Author inquiries and mail orders:
Finishing Line Press
P. O. Box 1626
Georgetown, Kentucky 40324
U. S. A.

Table of Contents

I

Near-Death Experience 1
Selling Home 2
The Crab Nebula 3
Medicinal Marijuana 4
Our Former House 5
A Neutropenic Romance 6
A Damaging Admission 7
Hamlet in the Cancer Ward 8
The Butterfly Effect 10
The Poisoned Well 12
Images of an Impostume 14
On "Standing Up to Cancer" 15
On "Cheating Death" 16
On "Making Sense of Cancer" 17
Relapse 18
Bad Blood 19
Brother and Border 20
Asleep in a Bright House 21
Blood Palimpsest 22
The One Who Cured Me 23
Prolepsis 24
Grotesque 26
Tempest 27
Side FX 28
Psychomachia 30
The Sputum Spectrum 32
BMTU 5771 34
Systole, Asystole, Diastole 36
Storming the Food Court (With King Lear) 37
My Vietnam War Movie 38
A Problem for the Dietitian 40
Mephitic 42
Something Out of Goya 43
The 6 Million Dollar Man 44
The Damaged Monster 46
The Uncanny Valley 48
A Stony Shed 49
I Have a Greedy Destiny 50

II

I Chose to Live 53
Decimated 54
Breezeway 55
First Shower After 57
Survivor 59
Miraculated 60
Singularity 61
Post-Traumatic Stress, Reordered 62
Graft-Versus-Host 63
Genetically Modified Organism 64
The Wrong Alternatives 65
Zeugmatic 67
Catachrestic 68
Rash 70
A Modest Dose of Morphine 71
Chronicle 72
Double Agent 73
The Gentle Pushers 75
Hellacious 77
Farewell My Medicine 78
Cogito Roulette 80
The Day I Took No Pain Medication 81
Sleeping Naked 82
Atrophy Wife 83
Hibernal 84
The Order of the Blue Pill 86
At the Last Reckoning 87
A Withering Gaze 88
A Choking Hazard 89
Reflux 90
A Convalescent's Railway Journey 92
Seven-Year Ache 93
Peregrine 94
My Niece's Theory of Ghosts 95
My Mask 97
Anemone 98
Retrospective 100
No Calvary 102
Returning from My Latest Infusion 104
The Forms 105
Morning Glory 106

About the Author 107

*This book is dedicated to my mother,
Susan Buchanan (née Castle),
who died from complications of malignant B-cell lymphoma
in December 2021.*

chi·me·ra
noun
1   a: a fire-breathing she-monster in Greek mythology having a lion's head, a goat's body, and a serpent's tail
           b: an imaginary monster compounded of incongruous parts
2   an illusion or fabrication of the mind; especially: an unrealizable dream
3   an individual, organ, or part consisting of tissues of diverse genetic constitution

I

Near-Death Experience

strangely foretold
beyond the plaid curtains
of my grandparents' last house
where I was threatened
by the bad taste
of my native decade

pathetic fallacies of the seventies
imagined just outside the window
malevolence internalized
domesticated reveries
of a gothic apocalypse

mechanisms reproduced
that took a little boy as their hostage
and then lost interest
in the ransom notes
he tried for hours to recompose

a trivial nightmare ending in tears
because the advance
he had made to death
had been ungraciously refused

Selling Home

cut your losses
as short as you can
the tiny place
where you grew up
was gone
long before
it was disowned
you sold it out
by knowing better
by leaving town
by living larger
than its little rules
had room for
by getting bored
with the games it hid
in child-sized cupboards
made of thin plywood
it was only ever yours
while you took it
all for granted
possessiveness
comes in retrospect
a hunger
for the unreal
estate of youth
soon forms a second thought
after the small property
is bought
by a new family
starting up
the narrow path
to the threshold of hope
their plans so tall
they forget to stoop

The Crab Nebula

it appeared like a new day star in Taurus
a sudden, illustrious guest on my PET scan
a fractal spun from a spider web
a ball of yarn coming apart at light speed
a remnant of a thousand-year-old supernova
visible to the naked eyes of Chinese
astronomers for more than 100 days
only outshone by the moon in the night sky
driven by one of the first known pulsars
an expanding neutron star
spinning at a rate of 30 times per second
emitting radiation in optical, radio,
gamma, and x-ray wavelengths
my cancer had run out of fuel and collapsed
pulled into its core by its own gravity
then was sent back out far beyond my
or anyone's imagination
exploded by orders of magnitude
through my oncologists' binoculars
looking for a predicted returning
bright comet adjacent to Aldebaran
near the belt of Orion, inside of the bull
not moving, so not a comet at all
eleven light years in diameter
a crust of fragments and filaments
containing ionized gases: hydrogen,
helium, oxygen, ion, sulfur, nitrogen, neon
a trail of untold energies and blinding
ever-accelerating aftershocks
and echoing blowback from that first tumor
the slight opacity in my left lung
a vague feeling that something was wrong
with a crenellated shell in my hand
on an island in the Pacific ocean

Medicinal Marijuana

with only leeches
to keep us warm
we lingered
in the lethal
antechambers
reserved for stoners:
rented, rec,
or waiting rooms
foundational spaces
of specious visions
the soft oppression
of senses in tingling
thrall to a romantic
chemical blessing
anticipating
the malaise
that would one day
legitimize
our distant ease

Our Former House

I miss that inconvenient space—
our derelict neighbors
the endless repairs
the attic with obvious traces of mice
the bedroom that our girls had to share
though one wasn't sleeping
the improvised plumbing
and cracked foundation
hassles with the bankrupt contractor
over an addition we couldn't afford
the single bathroom with no locks
on the janky doors
the baby-gate system tumbling down
the steepest, narrowest staircases
found this side of feudalism
the tiny kitchen with the leaky oven
whose disassembled, irreplaceable
parts would cover entire floors
the windows askew and insecure
taped-over frames for escaping air
the whole place a barely latent disaster—
because when we lived there
I didn't have cancer

A Neutropenic Romance

She is older, yes, but none the worse
for that. Her gray hairs burnish the rest
of her chestnut *chevelure*. Her everyday life,
whatever its petty irritations
contains a richness, a strain of soundness
that mourns but opens itself to experience.

I, whom sickness has made hairless,
aged and puerile, try to conceal
my weakening body, surprise her with sterile,
phantasmal desire. I must risk my whole frail being
to touch her normal, indelicate beauty,
frisk her nakedness for invisible menace.

Sometimes I wonder if this is not
the real meaning of death at last:
the irresistible embrace
of someone you admire and trust.

A Damaging Admission

In a hospital you can walk right in—
if you act like you already belong

they admit you. There's no privacy, but a home
truth sinks in immediately: every vein

is a vulnerability, links back to mom-
entum leeching you bonewards a tube at a time.

All this in the face of everything else—
the purposeful nurse, the constructive forces

plumbing, replenishing, pointing to health
and sympathizing with the ongoing crisis

of being born, growing up, getting old,
moving through places that throb to your need.

The delirium comes when your uncontrolled
body gains an awareness that something outside

itself is producing a synthesis,
putting your life to unconscious use

and breeding a monstrous artifice,
an invited guest: a child or a corpse...

Hamlet in the Cancer Ward

The unwritten poem of my desire cannot save you, even if you were finally done with your terrible treatment and in remission. There is no cure worth the mention no matter how long my tragic pantomime endures, or how many deliberations it takes to return a verdict of pain and degradation. Guilt is another form of resolution, unfair as it seems, implying a karmic justice beyond human comprehension and therefore comically divine. What did I ever do to deserve such a dreary company? The Player King wears a long cloak, spotless and white, and sticks to his straight-man script, a diction full of dire jargon and deferrals. Deference is not his strong suit, yet he bows to the statistically probable death he holds like a dusty prop, at a safe but scrutinized distance, just like you-know-who. His imitation of me, however, is nowhere near convincing enough; he is part of the problem I'm trying to solve, though he'll never admit it. I know he knows it, too, in his overstrained heart of hearts; we are all heart-sick, and heartily sick of hearing about it. Still, don't lose faith (whether bad or good) in the science he stands for. There is nothing likelier in any story, let alone mine. Tell it to the orderlies, if they still have those. Don't blame heredity for your missed chances, and don't spend your inheritance wishing that it had never happened. There is a reason for everything, especially for gratuitous suffering. Just don't expect me to know what it is. We are trapped in a play with no adequate cause for its final solutions. Concentrate, dammit! You never know when you'll be asked to perform this whole act, word for word, all over again. Name and birth date. Death date unknown but coming soon to a YouTube station near you. Baroque flute music might follow you home from this crowded last recourse. Please press "1" to confirm your attendance at the expected disappointment. You see? I know all these technologies and how they denature us, which is why I even bother having a phone, despite the fact that I was plenty phony already. Let's get up and circulate, shall we? Let's spread our infectious, affected gaiety while it lasts. You might even be able to shit again if you walk around and ease gravity into your bowels. Let the other patients see you dancing with your IV tower. Graceful or clumsy, it doesn't matter, as long as you stay on this cloistered floor. The food court is too full of formalities—chewing and swallowing, let alone leaving room for the breathtaking conversations—better stay where they can manage your silence and lack of appetite. Or am I projecting? Never mind. One day you will understand. I have been what you now seem, and I can counterfeit all the bad dreams you can imagine. Ennobled by shame and its endless rescheduling, I claim no right to save or end any life, whether yours, mine. or the parasite's that threatens to be everybody's deadly frenemy. Which is to say that we are getting right back to where we started from, a new acquaintance to be forgotten in a crisis and only recalled from an envious distance if we survive long enough to refresh our screens of sentiment. Curious yet negligent, I trail a breadcrumb's worth of hints behind me as I leave the stage I carry with me for such occasions. Casual yet diligent, I step aside for life to pass—raving mad and strapped to a gurney, a pregnant teen, if I had to guess.

The Butterfly Effect

pregnant this time
with her own future
a 74 year-old mother of two
wife of more than fifty years
grandmother of five
considers pain
before and after
the bone marrow biopsy
nothing like childbirth
nowhere near as wrenching
or as rewarding
a breeze in fact
thanks to her midwife
the junior hematologist
who dug a needle
into her hip
it's easier for the elderly
she tells her son
who's had two of his own
but he wants to give her
another way
to face her fears
with a metaphor
he says that cancer
will help her shed
the dead cells
of her outer layer
that chrysalis will yield
a lighter being
a delicate fluttering
feeling
a gratitude sweeter
than suffering's sour taste
can imagine
a burst
of heightened color
fragile and febrile

a species more rare
than any she has ever
brought forth before
a next herself
to test the air
wholly vulnerable
as all newborns are

The Poisoned Well

What kind of
thirst
would it take
to dunk
a bucket into
this ground to drink
the poison
welling up
within me?

Contamination
so obscene
must warn off all
but a damaged
mind
or a savaged
throat
already ripped
and bleeding out.

This rounded
frame
is an exit wound
made by a hidden
weapon
a dug-in deceit
a firm conviction
full of fatal
contradictions.

This sink of festering
corruption
is deep to the ear
and clean
to the eye
but unwholesome
to digestion.

I should die
were I
the victim
and not the sign
of horrid
welcome.

Images of an Impostume

i

Awake with the scandalous certainty
that certain printouts have proven to me:
someone on my ward is a fraud,
traceable to this exact address
from suburban Minneapolis,
where he played cancer and fought God.

ii

The body that was sick has died;
the rest of me now has it made.

Recovery is an inheritance
of finally limited mischance,
mortality a statistic no more
dangerous than driving a car.

Not back to normal yet, I have firm
excuses for staying clear of harm.

I am safe among these irrelevant matters,
afloat in the mind's untroubled waters.

iii

This half-full plastic urinal;
a twisted tankard of sour red ale.

On "Standing Up to Cancer"

Cancer is not your standard bully;
it will not back down if confronted
with sufficiently brave defiance.

It doesn't have a nervous system
to mobilize or sympathize.

The only martial arts it knows
are patience, stealth and resilience.

It turns our best aggressions against us,
gives us back our toxic adrenaline
with an endless creative vengeance.

If it ever suspects what a nemesis
it has in us, it will only redouble its effortless
mutable viciousness; and if we speak
of battles, it is only to salve
our conscience about those we couldn't save.

The scars we show are of amputations,
mutilations and cauterized wounds
incurred on our reckless crusade to survive,
not souvenirs of actual wars.
                            But
what beast, ensnared, would not sacrifice some
bloody part of itself to escape martyrdom?

On "Cheating Death"

I gave it the squarest deal I could
a lengthy opportunity
to cash in at the roulette wheel
or at the slots
where the coins poured out
for countless others.
I nearly went bankrupt
feeding it chips
but somehow missed
the expected payout.
I even reserved
a special chair
at the blackjack table;
I wore my best casino suit
and daylong shades;
I doubled down
on my chamber pot,
came up with the same old
four-flushing farts
in my adult diapers;
I lost all shame
and bathroom manners
but somehow
every game was rigged.
I did not cheat death;
it cheated me
of my rightful
valedictory bucketful
of spoils from the place
with no clocks or natural light,
where the dutiful croupier
kept his thumb on the button
to ensure that the longest odds
were also the most agonizing;
inevitably, they favored the house
and made my bad beat
feel even worse.

On "Making Sense of Cancer"

not senseless
but innocent of intention
full of physical
stimulation
withholding value
judgements on
all that for the moment
of pain or pleasure
and their terrible
interdependence
only numb
at extremities
and even that
callous magic
takes time
I wear the meaning
of what is perceived
as suffering
like a sleeveless gown
suitable for
a romantic evening
or an IV
in a hospital room
this is no rational event
but it doesn't
elude the mind
for very long
I am sensible
of my predicament
if not of all
its details and outcomes
I prove its data
on my pulse
not even sleep
will bring it peace

Relapse

who hasn't gone back
on a path
on a pledge
to get better somehow
at hobbies or health
or kicking a habitual urge?
don't let them convince you
that you have failed chemo
those arrows of blame
must revert to their bow
even if there is no more
treatment possible
at this time
imagine tomorrow
as a different paradigm
with an experimental
hollow into which
your body may fit
unbeknownst to anyone
even the trusted minds
of sage and scientist
can be blown away
like the last straw
that you must grasp at
as if all our lives
depended upon
the sight of your singular
irreplaceable
silhouette
against a wall

Bad Blood

the rivalries inside
my family
are bloodier than
mere consanguinity
authorized
there is no love lost
in such tight circles
it just turns nasty
we call each other
by the names
we have learned to hate
leukemia at first
then three-times cursed
lymphoma
violent grudges
that last a lifetime
contagious as
retaliation
or snide remarks
on a long vacation
where everybody gets sick
of everybody else
and themselves
we are our best victims
our deepest
hurt feelings
keep us hemorrhaging
empathy and envy
for generations
as though our malady
were more important
to us than mortality
all the sins that run
through our veins
both typical and original
coagulate at last into clots
like wadded Kleenex
on weeping hearts

Brother and Border

We never rested till they had built
a wall between us. A family resemblance,
polarized, sent us spinning across
the vast expanse of self-centeredness
to different countries. We weren't enemies
except when we were caught in the wrong place.
A biting remark left a scar on my face
but it was really more like a kiss
that had misfired, a flag of truce
shot down at a checkpoint, mistranslated.
Now we are long-standing, faraway allies
with wives who, like embassies, keep us in touch
quite painlessly. Now and then we meet
in our children's neutral territories
and, instead of telling stories
of how atrociously we fought
we admire each other's formalities.
Our eyes lock in a strangers' salute.

Asleep in a Bright House

It is bright because
everyone can see in.

I am asleep because
I am determined
to be at ease
in this scattered sunlight.

My hand on the wall
recognizes its shape
too late.

I am talking
because I'm asleep.

Everyone can see in because
I am determined
to write
until the light is gone.

I will hide when
there is something to touch
instead of this glowing,
receding wall.

The sound of this being
becomes too much.

I wait for consciousness
to fall.

Blood Palimpsest

when his brother's stem cells go in
he is the only drowsy one
in the crowded isolation room
worn out by all the anticipation
the fluids and the Benadryl
he has the most peculiar dream:
his skin comes loose
and curls into scrolls
of brown papyrus
he writes his name
then watches it vanish
the next time he inscribes
a pseudonym
when that too is gone
he begins forging other signatures:
William Shakespeare
Emily Dickinson
when he wakes up
he is covered in red ink
a text he cannot believe
is his own

The One Who Cured Me

The one who cured me—killed me first—
The paradox was planned—
He brought my father back to life—
a sacrifice—exhumed—

I gave my only son to him—
He burned the infant bones—
a holocaust like Abraham's
smoldered—in my veins—

I sickened with this grisly physic—
offered punctured palms
for a salve—of fraternal love—
and he ordered—Cain's—

Prolepsis

a dead man before
I knew what had hit me
I woke up in advance
of my nightmare's
anticlimax
my winter thawed early
and left me in a puddle
of terrified memories
of what never happened
I tried fast-forwarding
to the last scene
but the fingers
that scrubbed me
rubbed it out
I am suddenly
out of step with my destiny
so far over my limit
I don't know how
or when to stop
things that are timely
and things that are not
(interventions and executions,
warnings and recriminations,
stitches and justifications)
they all look
the same to me
since I have imagined
where they are tending
a destination
we all see coming
and can't avoid
the ultimate word
we learn is an elegy
for the sensation
we have yet to find
in any object
the final simplicity

of a shortcut
in a dream
that gets to the best part
where you slay the enemy
you have just
discovered
for the first time

Grotesque

in a rancid grotto beneath
the burnished ruins of ancient Rome
they found two bodies
perversely joined together
half-lion, half man
an august astrological sign
dragged into the muck
of a human being reborn
out of season
with cancer ascendant
under Janus's fourfold gaze
and Damocles's single-edged sword
I was that chimerical twinned self
amazement incarnate
pinned down by my own
Herculean form
at the edge of a precipice
blind as a worm
and winged like a vampire bat
I lay in a windowful
of morning
like an angel overcome
with awareness of universal evil
and released to oblivion

Tempest

the clouds that shrouded us
drove us apart forever
not even our smartphones worked
in that absolute nightmare
I was cast away
to wait with a nursery
of flight attendants
one of whom tearfully
reassured me
that we would all
survive somehow
though the mainland
was invisible
and the hostile sky was
gathering fresh gray
squadrons of moisture
you were with your family
so my first call
was to my mother
to prepare her tactfully
for the all-but-official divorce
with no fault
but the San Andreas
rubbing tectonic
plates together
like god's own
overloaded dishwasher
flooding the kitchen
until no repairman
could stem the flow
of that wrathful water

Side FX

it's a sleazy B-movie
into which you've been cast
for a cameo role
by a famous director
before the auditions
have taken place
because you are special
or have specialized
in getting certain
dramatic effects
a character actor
with a tragic demeanor
who works cheap
and is right in line
with the studio's
low production values
you play the role
of the unlucky patient
the one to whom
all the bad stuff happens:
nausea, headaches,
sleeplessness, fever,
sweats, constipation,
irregular heartbeat
all the symptoms
they warn you about
before you sign
the legal disclaimer
that exculpates
the respected
script doctor
you make it, somehow
to the cheesy last scene—
unsteady recovery
played as redemption—
that you welcome
nevertheless

because it ends
like everything else
and maybe it's better
than the chance you missed
to star in your own
chemical bromance

Psychomachia

Mirtazapine and Ativan
two moody titans
come to blows
after many a covert
nightlong struggle
a battle in darkness
has awakened
to find the whole world
swarming with wartime
slogans and urgent
random memories
propaganda from
former allies
now apparently
hedging their bets
backing the prevailing drugs
to keep the peace
whenever it comes
self-deception
is the diplomacy
of the confused
and uninsured
I have finally
taken against me
because my delusions
refuse to stand guard
over a quiet death
misdiagnosed
and maladjusted
I am resisting
not being arrested
until it is much too late
for lack of a better word
I fight
the evil inside me
instead of resting
up till all hours

my thoughts conflicting
with each other
in quick succession
denying every proposition
both within
and without reason

The Sputum Spectrum

I must have
swallowed
one messed-up
rainbow
to cough up
all the colors I do

they may end
as they began
with candy apple
crimson and scarlet
then a rusty indigo

the grays
and greens are from
my sickest days
when I am glazed
and nausea-bound

the purples
and yellows are
bitter recoveries
masked with
an acrid chemical hue

the orange
is a vitamin agent
or sherbet's
acid afterglow

violet
is thrown up
violently
like a poisoned
bouquet

when I saw
straight red
that meant what
it said
and a nightlong
black puke
was all I knew

BMTU 5771

Sid ("The Kid") Crosby's golden goal;
Hunter Pence's bat shattering
into three pieces and dying a hero.

These were the pictures on the wall
when I, blind and distracted, tried to pull
my own plug.
    The beeping machine
wouldn't stop and I'd had enough.

Some sweet liquid spilled out
and my nurse was upset.
      I had rolled
in my own shit again.
      Somehow
there was barbed wire all over the vacant lot
in which I'd been trying to plant a garden.

The people on the cruise ship were fed up
with that fucked-up, endless regatta;
they licked red vomit from envelopes
and wanted more.
     Two medications met
in my brain and fought to a standstill;
waking delirium went on the record
sometime around two o'clock
in the morning.
    My very best symptoms
didn't quite match what they were
expecting.
   Another experience
lost its meaning in the wild, unfocused
light of the dawn.
     Nothing had changed
but my tubes and the temperature,
which was unbearable.

      I was a fire
smoldering in a pile of damp leaves
and flaking fungus.
      Neither alive
nor able to die in a recognized manner,
I became that unit's room number,
and was known as seventy-one thereafter.

Systole, Asystole, Diastole

I stole this system
of circulation
from another human body
robbed the grave
of my former self
to give my current incarnation
a second chance
at achieving a flat line
on the endlessly beeping screen
at my bedside
was almost gone
but ripped the missing vein
out of my brother's avatar
and grafted it in
to steady my breathing
ate the heart of the mutant twin
they grew in a bottle
and called it survival
caught my ghost
as it tried to depart
and beat it back to a wispy pulp
with my aggrieved
and grieving fist
against my tube-infected chest
emptied the chambers
of my gut
into the arteries of the bed
then after a deadly pregnant pause
lay back and let the shit roll in
from all directions
the muscle was numb
but my life resumed
at its blameless pace
unaware of this crime

Storming the Food Court (With *King Lear*)

unable to eat or sleep in his room he was wheeled out to contend with the fretful elements since it was raining he and his father awaited his brother who had gotten lunch at the cafeteria his darker purpose was to linger near the outdoor food court where no patients were allowed despite auricular assurance that he was not permitted to enter he cried in outrage, "Death to my state!"
suddenly touched with noble anger he performed his unsightly tricks and conjured from the pendulous air an act of darkness he foretold the cause of thunder that sent the legitimate diners to shelter so that no one was left to complain of how soon he became the comrade of the wolf and owl from that place he did no leading need though he was blind he seemed to see the things he did not he could smell the nearby pizza and his own gloved mortality he wanted to stop at the pharmacy but found that even an ounce of civet would not sweeten his imagination when finally the sunlight shone that was no good divinity he was informed that the atrium was off-limits his newly circumscribed realm awaited him in an elevator and he wept for the man of salt he had become he knew he stumbled when he saw but could not free his brain from madness by that briefly lucid fiat he railed, a child-changed father, at some missing pairs of socks and cursed his kin for not bringing them in the heaviness of his sleep they had put fresh garments on him to replace those he had fouled in his nightlong extremity when he was hovelled with swine in the musty straw they had taken him out of the grave to mock his tarnished image with tokens of belated love and wronged him with bitter untrustworthy medicine he thought of many who had desperately foredone themselves and others who were unjustly dead the wonder was he endured so long and yet he wished for one more minute with her whose faithful heart had burst smilingly and who in kindness brought him some untasted soup and finally had undone a button

My Vietnam War Movie

another shot in the fevered dark

another backward stab at sleep

my bed was a disputed bridge
between two fires
where mortars raged all night
and only the dawn brought stillness

on my right side lay a jungle of trip wires
and tubes leading up to a swiveling tower
whose loaded guns aimed medication
indiscriminately at insurgents
and the innocent

on my left was a ridge of mountains
housing alternate intelligence
a neutral tribe with music and food
on offer for when the conflict resolved
into psychedelic introspection

I loved the violence but hated the war
with its bureaucratic moralism

I wanted to die but not before
I had claimed my victory
over that state of emergency

I wanted a premature declaration
to authorize one last celebration
fireworks at the surrendered stage

a charge of the helicopter brigade
to airlift me from the rooftop pad
of the hospital

before the horde
of rushing admirers could converge
and destroy me for good

in all that confusion
I had learned
how to play a deranged god

A Problem for the Dietitian

the strange spikiness
of a naked saltine
in a raw
parched mouth
mumbles
that sound like mine
from an echo chamber
a mile away
noncommittal
as to the nutritional
value of chewing
on a thistle
with no intention
of swallowing
a problem for the dietician
to resolve with
indigestible jargon
calories counted
and discounted
every Gatorade flavor
invented has already tried
and failed to replenish
my carbohydrates
I find myself damaged
beyond refreshment
I have slipped past
the clutches of appetite
only to wash up nauseated
before a tray table
where chicken soup
bluntly refuses
to slurp itself
and the endless churning
in my entrails
is fed by a broth
that my bones
have boiled up

a noxious brew made
from eye of newt
and tongue of frog
into rotten umbilical stew
while I slept

Mephitic

a simple lit match
dissipates
mephitic vapors
this cold night

not the gut-ache
memories
of endless fetid
agonies

the stench of toxic
swallowed death
amid the miracle
of rebirth

women too
give of their worst
in offering
deliverance

the light they strike
redeems the earth

how soon my pain
burns through
this gift

I curse all those
fastidious fools
whose cure has burst
my visceral urge
to mourn the dirt
I sit atop

they have corrupted
my sunken
heart

Something Out of Goya

a naked
mutilated man
impaled upon a tree
may be a heroic
attempt at grafting
a dying species
upon a living
and not the warning
it appears to be

    after a bloody battle
    as an exemplary
    nightmare
    to show that further
    resistance is futile
    that the dark forces
    will always prevail
    that the proof of this
    is atrocity

perhaps I am
just the one
to see beauty
in this failed arboreal
experiment
this could be
the warped mirror
I have been seeking
in the fascinating
disasters of war

    like the smoke
    of a killed village
    arising just behind
    a bomber pilot's
    shrugging shoulders
    the instant before
    he crashes his plane

The 6 Million Dollar Man

Everything happened
in slow motion
with a primitive sound effect.
My change was induced
by a whirring engine.
An experiment
made me
a new, whole man
with bionic blood cells
enhanced immune
capabilities
adamantine routines
and a fluid exoskeleton.
They reinforced
my hollowed-out bones
with fresh DNA
from a distant twin
automaton.
I am so deep in
the government's debt
that I owe my awesome
power for good
to anybody
wearing white
or red
or blue
for the rest
of this lifetime
and the next.
Tooled up
and totaled
in the same scripted
episodes
I watched as a kid,
I lurch from one
expensive stunt
to another

wearing a younger man's suit
of body armor;
my organs a treasure
so valuable
they are worth
all this
torture.

The Damaged Monster

Can a monster
be damaged further
than its baseline
deviation accounts for?

Might not the flaw
in my scaly
armored skin
infect me with a new
mutation
that actually
turns me back
into a human?

Or are my injuries severe
enough that
no change of mine
can remedy them?

Could I merely
be playing possum
in the process of
becoming something
they no longer recognize?

No such hybrid
of the future
and the immemorial past
has ever survived
beyond a few hours.

Someone will always
kill it or force it
to murder itself,
to finish the torture.

They cannot be witness
for very long
to pain they do not
understand.

The Uncanny Valley

I have taken up residence
in a deep discomfort zone
just human enough
to make people squirm
but not so lifelike
as to disarm
my voice has taken on
modulations I can neither
accept nor disown
an obsolete robot
who offers his hand
in tardy greeting
or premature parting
I turn the wrong way
on a dime
and end up junked
beside the freeway
with all the other
homunculi

A Stony Shed

astonished
to find I am alive
let alone
with a roof
over my head
I wonder about
what kind of building
I seem to have
inhabited
almost a hut
of earth
with roots for rafters
a ceiling of dirt
and floor made up
of moss and mud
but closer to
a rabbit warren
in the air
with one exception
in the middle
there is a structure
about whose purpose
I speculate
it might be
of a religious nature
but I am forbidden
knowledge of that
it barely fits
my unclad body
an iron maiden
before the invention
of ductile metal
or the concept
of the undead
not quite
a palace of bone
more like
a stony shed

I have a greedy destiny

I have a greedy destiny
that will not find its way;
it charts a course I cannot trace
no matter how I spy.

I followed it till, threat by threat,
it cornered me one day.
It disappeared—but everywhere
it stared at me. An eye

depicted on an antique canvas
winked, and I could see
some subtle fool behind the arras
imitating me.

I stabbed, and pulled the veined veil sideways;
everybody knew
the thing I'd killed was merely mercy—
God was mortal too.

My soul made many graceful farewell
curtsies, but denied
the leave I humbly craved of her—
she would not say goodbye.

No one would guess what brought me through
that doubly damnèd day:
so helpless was my selfish fate
I couldn't even die.

II

I Chose to Live

I chose to live—I had no choice—
Death beckoned me—to stay—
His terms were dear—and to refuse
was voiceless—agony—

Through endless nights did he upon
my patience much presume—
At length I laid a beseeching head
on his unrestful arm—

and I confessed a blissful wish
but he could grant me—none—
our nuptial sleep—like fever—broke—
or lilacs—from a tomb—

Decimated

When a Roman legion
performed badly in battle
the troops would remain
at strict attention
while every tenth man
was slaughtered.

That disgraceful
terrified discipline
served their future
commanders well.

How stand I, then
who have been plucked
to safety while nine
of my comrades
were killed summarily
by the extreme disease
that threatened me?

Was it my own cowardice
that gave me life
at their expense?

What part of me shall be
put to the sword
to slake the thirst
of that vengeful guard?

Breezeway

between North
and South buildings
I was wheeled
on daily outings
to listen for
a change in the air
from inside my tent
of yellow garments
while the traffic
was passing
or even when
my daughters
were visiting
every day it was
too bright for me
to see anything
but I could perceive
an easing of
the pressure
inside my shut-in
silence
I never prayed
but praised the space
around me
the widening world
was peaceful again
somehow
from where I
was sitting
postponing the painful
stumble to health
when I'd shuffle along
on someone's arm
until I could stand
to hear myself
breathing
under my mask

accept what living
had become
for me
at that time
in that drafty alley
between hope
and shame

First Shower After

I sat in my stall and rubbed
the dead skin
from my neck
it came away like globs
of rice pudding
some patient prankster had
slathered there
waiting for water
to turn me into a sloppy
quivering mess.
My daily caregiver averted
her eyes
my own were nowhere
shrouded
in a filthy curtain
and left for a miracle
to redeem.
I took my baptism as a blessing
scalding salt poured
into the wounds
on either side
of my cathetered heart.
She tried to cover my chest
with tape and Saran Wrap
as if packing a gift
or a piece of public art.
It was hardly a prophylactic
against the infection
that would bring me back
to the hospital
like an undelivered parcel.
Such a far-fetched suffering
could hardly expect to feel at home
even in a private bathroom
naked except
for disfigurement
and a chestful of tubes

they hung like medals
on a veteran of the BMTU
who hadn't bathed in more
than three months
and who almost dissolved
in that stall
that she knew.

Survivor

still available
when they call roll
in the classroom
where I am one more
remedial student
a slower learner
of the usual platitudes
sitting up straight
and keeping my bathroom
breaks short
but present, goddammit
they write my name down
every morning
and send me home
with Lord only knows
what snide remarks
in my permanent record
what a joke to think
I was once a teacher
doling out grades
for good behavior
better not to remind
anyone that I know
how it feels
to earn a diploma
so nobody minded
if I worked from home
or simply absented
myself for months
I keep my head down
and don't care whether
they give me an "A"
or call me a dunce
I am here with my body
in stubborn attendance

Miraculated

once more amazed
by the state I'm in
there are smudges
on the doors of perception
but they have at least
been turned to glass
every morning
I bump my nose
quite painfully on them
tricked afresh into
stepping through my limits
I eventually find the one
I shattered when
I was out of my mind
and retrace my steps
from the day before
when I went exploring
the sobbing air
clings to my body
the deaths of so many
echo in chorus
crying for more
and better mourners
I crush my usual little tear
and finally tear myself away
with a respectful formality
such are the difficult rituals
of those who find
they are miracles

Singularity

my single
wrinkled fingernail
points towards
the old age
that my whole
distorted, tender
body interrogates
from a deliberate
loveless distance
striated
and significantly
warped
it warns off
those who might
otherwise warm
to a tremulous touch
accuses my
abusive fate
of stressing me out
beyond the tipping
ticklish edge
of human endurance
this shows me how
every bone bends
under the pressure
of probing life
in a malleable casing
I will dispose of
after just
one use

Post-Traumatic Stress, Reordered

to will an eternal recurrence of this
would be a kind of insanity
but it is nonetheless possible
I could have done without the c-diff
and the stodgy hospital food
but my life at its very worst
was at least engagingly awful
those who set my dumpster ablaze
included a few awesome pyrotechnics
they were the rightly trashy fireworks
after that long and tedious fuse
was so tortuously consumed
just to realize that I was there
while all the crazy bad shit went down
as if I had consented preemptively
to such a spectacular fecal display
imposes a certain serenity
and yes I would live it all over again
as if I had known of no other way

Graft-Versus-Host

another attempt at writing the fable
of the grasshopper and ant
will only yield the same old moral
self-satisfaction of the useful
at the expense of the beautiful
so let me try a different route

I speak of harsh intolerance
amid a doomed and decadent people
a tightly fascinated whir
of helicopters strafing the air-
conditioned suburbs

a gang of youthful hoodlums
handing out contamination
in the form of handgun licenses
to suicidal veterans

these are the dualities
that express the opposition
in my own obstructed bloodline

the knot at the base
of the expanding universe
we call the future

I will never get beyond
this divided original ground
my rebirthday overturned
into an all-hell's-broken-out
along the once-bisected commute

and now the traffic of my blood
invents collisions so absurd
no warning could have made
this difference
less agonized or absolute

Genetically Modified Organism

one part of me
does not like the others
senses a separate origin
elsewhere
hurts what hinders
its self-expression
saws at the quick
of my fingernails
has a bitter distaste
for my tongue
drops hints
of distemper
into my liver
leaves faint-inducing
traces of arsenic
in my kidneys
hates my guts
with a torrid passion
keeps me safe
from a still worse
enemy
knows I depend
on its hostility
loves me
in spite of everything
like an envious
younger brother
who plots his revenge
through a two-way mirror
and watches me
where I blindly suffer
the life-giving
adrenaline
of his anger

The Wrong Alternatives

fight or flight
is no choice
for a human being
to have to make
it's been two years
I'm still struggling
to accept
what happened to me
less than a mile away
from where I sit
I never thought
I'd have returned
to this safe distance
I lost every battle
and somehow
survived the war
I never even ran away
or tried playing dead
though I lay inert
long enough to fool
the nervous junior officer
finishing off
the enemy wounded
nor was I charged
with cowardice
though I fainted at
every new opportunity
for intelligent consent
I even tagged along
with that stupid
cavalry assault
always loyal
to faulty poetry
a monster perhaps
but one with a certain
historical imagination
I chose both instincts

to follow blindly
into the breach
where they tore my body
and bore it back to me
illusions intact
having gotten its feculent
whiff of glory

Zeugmatic

they marked me out for special treatment
       with a different pen each day
traced the outlines of my organs
       and my disease's evanescence
gave me hope
       and a donor's stem cells
put me under observation
       and anesthetic to prolong
       the tantalizing prophetic charm
sent me home with a thousand instructions
       and a feeling that I was to blame
       for the pain of my self-division
as if I had birthed a bomb
       and not a pink delicious infant
brought me news of danger again
       and yet another antithesis
       to keep me blindfolded and breathless
held my hand in a distant city
       and my future a grave uncertainty
proved a loyal friend at least
       and that my fears were finally false
left me a box full of medication
       and as if in the wild abandoned

Catachrestic

the proper name
by which I was known
has been reclaimed
for another being

a new idea
demanding a form
however tortured
is its beginning

I give myself up
to that hazardous
happening
as to a needful destiny
already working
through my organs

a forced metaphor
of my choosing
and bringing forth
but not mine to change

a killing literalism
eluding its diagnosis
to assume
chimerical shapes
I call survival
for lack of better
terminology

from now on
it must go down
as the undeathing
I have willed
into words
where nothing
similar was imagined
before

a sound to breathe back
to the listening air
beyond my
inexistent
and limitless power

Rash

I want to scrape this savaged skin
wash its hot mess off the bone
slash the prickly underbrush
to clear a path for a nuclear balm
that peels the atom's irritations
into fiery smithereens
destroy the crawling enemy lurking
in the epithelial layer
drop hellfire into spider holes
along this embattled ridge of pores

though I know that this violence
will only succeed in
spreading the terrors
that soon reform into resistance
bristling on my back and shoulders
there is no cure or suppression
only rationales for appeasement
after agonizing hours
of frustrated commando raids
painful reconciliation
to fresh reprisals on all sides

A Modest Dose of Morphine

my Orphic metamorphosis
has left me with much discomfort
and yet with some powerful allies
whom I keep under lock and key
for just such mythic emergencies
as last night's splitting stomach
phobic about insomnia
I declared an urgent need
and conjured a dose of the distilled
spirit of winged Morpheus
with a snub-nosed plastic syringe
but that fantastical maker of dreams
offered no memorable gesture
no tantalizing scenario
no Sisyphean obligation
born of childhood's rich confusion
no suggestive substitution
in the aphrodisiac lingo
of my heteronormative boredom
no Daedalian pseudonym
under which I could become
someone wiser than I am
nothing but an empty head
on a familiar simple pillow
therefore morphine I must praise you
as the greatest god of all

Chronicle

like clockwork the syndrome returns
the red goosebumps on the underarms
the itch around the sunken hips
the spoiling hurt inside the gut
the torn third nipple that houses my port
they all add up to what I've got
now every night
a boring story I check for consistency
how raw is the skin?
how thick is the scab?
when did I notice and what was the last?
the questions too are less acute
they probe the pain, do not penetrate it
they simply add another layer
to the silt of a stagnant river
time itself seems to go nowhere
following circadian nightmares
into ever-descending circles
like the nadir of news cycles
each report a little more horrible
in its suggestion of paralysis
of everything but the toxic wastes
of time and space
where we suffer the truth

Double Agent

unmasked
my pain wears a thin
fixed grimace
that also faces
an inward awareness
disease is my only way
not to die
if you want
to think of it as life
then so be it
I tend to refer to this
state as undeath
a double negation
that pits one ill feeling
against another
this twinship conditioning
what would otherwise
seem like mere secrecy
but get me talking
and I will reveal
all the dire plots
still hatching
the ancient moles waking
from patient surveillance
to ruthless sabotage
manifesting themselves
in their once-numb
surroundings
mounting an overdue
insurrection
against the sovereign body
with drones and cyber-terror
touching off
tactical violence everywhere
with chaos as its ultimate goal
and stopping at nothing
short of anarchy

all this subversion
contained in one cell
already dividing
to conquer the world

The Gentle Pushers

betrayed by
the happy accident
of having killed off
the pain for the moment
I am the charmed
adept of a life
unthinkable
without addiction
the gentle art
of adulteration
helps me smooth out
the contradictories
at the root of
my nervous system
of rationales
so many reasons
I have for living
do not suffice
without the remedies
helpfully provided
by the physicians
who embrace the raw
fact of survival
with no regard
for the awful interval
between each rescue
each fresh procedure
of the fascinating
bureaucracy
totally preoccupied
with denying
the truth of their state
to the gradually dying
unaware that we
are all just chasing
the dragon
of an ultimate degradation

the consummation
of just the right chemical
at the defensible interval
slowly bending
denatured desire
into a sharp need
only they can fulfill

Hellacious

if you doubt the veracity
of my tales
from the underground
I can only offer my
very own body
as evidence of
what is to be found
on the other side
of its porous surface
I was simply
turned inside out
and left to rot
my organs on show
it was one hell
of a spectacle
or so I am informed
every day
when I prise myself
out of my death-bed
and try to look
at myself
in the mirror
I run my eyes over
the third-degree burns
beneath
the epithelial layer
my skin is
a translucent fiction
I wear so as not
to dissolve
in that puddle of fire
they cast me in
confident I'd return
to my adolescent
mess of a room
in something akin
to angelic form
but the morning light
shows what I really am

Farewell My Medicine

saying goodbye
to prednisone
is a painful affair
like leaving a lover
who alternately soothed
and stimulated
whom all your friends
warned you against
but on whom you doted
an intoxicating
nonentity
you nevertheless
depended upon
when your senses
and membranes
were inflamed
when desire could
find no other way
the addictive squeeze
you must kick
cold turkey
before the massive
organ failure
before the porous
bones can shatter
before you inherit
another disaster
high-maintenance flirt
you will never master
you son of a bitch
who nursed you
like a mother
then cursed you
like a vindictive father
and at whom
you will gaze
the next time

they walk past
with incredulous lust
and dumb-assed
tenderness

Cogito Roulette

I think therefore I aim and fire
at the general space of my awareness
not knowing if my luck will hold
if brain death would be bad or good

I have spun the karmic wheel
in search of an eternal fate
the curt verdict of a pistol
with five soft clicks and a single missile
that promises sudden Armageddon

otherwise my search for a unified being
with body and mind accepting each other
must continue out of range

I do not actually own a revolver
only an endless supply of pills
to launch at shadows beyond the wall
of consciousness where my health lies prone
and praying for rescue or a stray bomb
to end the nightlong sniping from nowhere

I find myself on both sides of a border
an idle forefinger probes my temple
for a way to soothe the pressure
some system of knowledge to simplify
this painfully stark duality

The Day I Took No Pain Medication

On the day I took no pain medication
nothing terrible actually happened
that hadn't occurred a million times before:
the poor, imprisoned by endless war,
soiled their threadbare comforts with fear;
the great renewed their compulsive demands
for austerity in everyone else;
the sick were treated and mistreated
according to the latest accepted
well- or not well-intentioned malpractice;
the pills and liquids that held me hostage
let me out for a breath of fresh air
and even took off the blindfold for
a few blurry photogenic moments
later to be used in yet more ransom notes
from the underground;
the nonstop propaganda of pain
continued, of course, spreading lies around
my publicized, politicized body.
By the time all the opiates had worn off
there were no sensations left
except for the traces of self-contradiction
at the core of my organism,
the indivisible self that holds
despite the nakedness of its disease,
the self-evidence of its polarized
and warring factions, the rift it denies.

Sleeping Naked

wanting nothing between
these sheets and my disease
I make a last decision
to sleep naked is one way
of facing the divine
preserved as if in amber
like Pharaoh in a tomb
I slap on moisturizer
to dull the itching brain
for a journey into darkness
my organs in a bowl
that sits atop my nightstand
like ballast for my soul
I dim the glowing membrane
they flayed off when I fell
out of my drunken sailboat
into this whirling pool
I close the painful eyes
that showed me what was hidden
and slowly realize
unconsciousness is heaven
so why not be reborn
make scarring of the skin
a sacred mutilation
that promises return
the hands that healed a rash
now burn, intangible
as scratch marks on the walls
show love implacable
and if this shameless pose
seems desperate, recall
the chafing that disarmed you
so you could touch what's real

Atrophy Wife

she leans on the table
and strains to assemble
a recognizable
human body
from the collection
of parts I have dumped
on its cushioned surface
she works at the edges
that ought to fit
together but don't
trying vainly
to sort out
the vestigial muscles
from the protruding bones
to tickle the slack
tendons back
into clinging position
to see if
some pressure can
restore the old heartbeat
engage the damaged
knee-jerk reflex
recoil the spring
in my ankles
give me the strength
to run
for a few strides
as if for a prize
she is pledged
to this exercise
does what she can
because she must
because it may bring
the piece she's missing
from where it's been hiding
the next part of both
of our lives
keeps us guessing

Hibernal

at first glance
the mind of winter
is breathtaking
in its calm
expansive candor
unmerciful but
not noticed until
it burns
the glaring sun conceals
its violence
setting foot
on a frozen lake
is treacherous
snow drifts over
all rifts and friction
bitter winds drive me
towards a forest
where I break
opaque panes of ice
find remnants
of a discarded dryad
Ursula Andress
pictured naked
dismembered by
self-hating desire
that tried to lose itself
in the cold air
of this cauterized
petrified maze
sheltered and
hidden from noonday's
tough breeze
a closer inspection
of any tree line
will reveal
such complications
as lying dormant

for months
won't resolve
the stiff-armed
gestures of
put-upon love

The Order of the Blue Pill

the blue pill waits alone
under lock and key
the high price of desire
means that I have to buy
in small quantities
even one rattling
in its plastic cartouche
is worth purchasing
20 bucks a pop
and that's with insurance
covering half
(suggestive gesture
understanding nod
wink to the willing
incapable flesh)
beneficial to health
at set intervals
O the once-widowed life
flourishing under
this hidden escutcheon
now I am ready
to be love's Freemason

At the Last Reckoning

a wet dream
at age forty-seven
an extra Christmas
after Rituxan
and god knows what else
leftovers from
yesterday's holiday feast
marriage vows
renewed in haste
at the therapist's office
a hit song
from my favorite
obsolete band
yet another new year
beyond the millennium
gratuitous grace
on the heels
of a coup
this much too
little comes
far too late
not to be welcomed
with delight
such unexpected
blessings count
double when
there was nothing
to bet on
let alone
to rely on
at the last reckoning

A Withering Gaze

the scars
on my forearms
remain unredeemed
although they healed
one itch at a time
they are still raw
to the touch
of the mind
strangely self-inflicted
stigmata born of
acute diarrhea
resting for weeks
on the commode
left a trace that
no cream wipes
could hide
a slow degradation
of the skin
that still burns
somewhere
inside my corneas
they cannot see me
for what I am
but keep the image
of what I was then
transposed on today
frame by frame
and I interpret
this memory as
compulsory prophecy
so I travel back
to that liminal room
to rescue what
was untouched
by my illness
and soon wither into
a skeleton

A Choking Hazard

I swallow hard
not impossible facts
but painful truths
about our disembodied
life

the very relationship
we deny
is stuck in its only
rightful place

a very long marriage
of equal minds
and many admitted
impediments

the injuries
picked up along the way
of separation and suffering
that stall in the craw

no longer unspoken
but undigested
unappetizing
resisting
any assimilation
for better or worse

unable to tell the difference
between sickness
and delicate health

afraid to breathe
too hard on the words
lest they break my throat
or choke us both

Reflux

the bad medicines
chase the good
medicines
down

the scorched
gorge rises
all over again

what tastes best
is not in
the best taste

we are what
kills us
and we eat
our waste

intoxicating
testosterone has
sired my daughters
harrowed my hairline

filmed
my eyes with
corrosive spume

no wonder it hurts
when I try
swallowing
this upsurge

desire
had better be choked
than strangle
the future

I offer my second
infancy
as martyred
impotence
from its cradle
of terror

A Convalescent's Railway Journey

The toughened windows on this train
make no effort to show me a good time.
The urban yardage they display is unadorned.
Buildings face the wrong way;
streets and highways run their own
intractable patterns beyond and between
green spaces growing alongside fences.
The shadows lean as the sunlight glances
with no grand design but motioning
counterpoints to my destination;
the transience of a restless arrival;
the jolting solipsism of travel
undertaken for its own sake.
I watch the living vistas swivel
as if I had paid for just this spectacular
unselfconsciousness of space
considered through a strict limit:
a trip of just three hours with multiple stops.
A dread-filled itinerant who has kept
to his schedule despite many interruptions,
I feel myself move from the safety I gripped
to fulfillment I've already overstepped
and yet enjoy in perfect security.
A daydream of distance encompasses me;
I trust my troubled eyes to close
on the functional temporary display
that will go on one day without me
or my fellow passengers. We will die
regardless of how justly we appraise
the speed of approach or the free-form delays
when a child-like eagerness greets our demise.
These seats will be needed;
this train goes both ways.

Seven-Year Ache

damn
they hurt me again
contrived to turn
the flaps of skin
dangling in my throat
from choking hazards
into gulps of pain
forgive me for not
gushing with gratitude
a long night of swallowing
gobbets of phlegm
not to mention
the ooze on the pillows
leaves me wondering
where it will end
this rising threshold
of my discomfort
how long an ache
will it take to drown
my few pleasures out?
my new slim pants fit
but what is the point
of the life
that inhabits them?
the cure for what's wrong
is a fresh inhibition
I strain to put in
a belated appearance
at the breakfast
I hope that no one will notice
I can't seem to eat
and must suffer to process

Peregrine

The falcon that nests
on top of this
medical building
is well known
for the bolus of bones
it casts on the lawn
of the Cancer Center
where I left my skin
or nearly.

The species is among
the most common
urban birds of prey.

No doubt one saw me
as I was wheeled out
below on just such
a bright spring day
barely three years ago.

I wonder what information
glinted
inside that nictitating
membrane.

Was I a target, or just
the rejected spoor
of a satisfied appetite?

Or was I a blind, bald
fallen fledgling
struggling, free
of its terrible height?

My Niece's Theory of Ghosts

every garage
with a broken window
every fence
with a missing board
is haunted
every roof
lacking a tile
houses an unquiet spirit
everything dilapidated
every doorstep
missing a brick
is a threshold
to another world
every tree
freshly pruned back
or with a branch
shorn off by a storm
is a portal
to a nightmare
where a vampire
lurks unseen
every person
lacking a limb
has one foot
in the afterlife
even a little girl
losing her two
front teeth
becomes a zombie
be careful
disrepair
is all around you
pointing the way
to the grave
and beyond
where our fixed
and decaying

flesh finds
its last crutch
and we finally
die

My Mask

my mask is cracked
and painted brown
and pink and yellow
it leaks hot tears
and stores up snot
for the choking hours
when the jammed pills
go in wrong
and the filter stops
taking oxygen
it foams faintly
around the ears
where I sprout
alarming hairs
it goggles like a pair
of crossed eyes
extrudes crystals
between lashes
behind lenses
fogged and scratched
prolongs my nose
into a double-headed
steam-dispensing engine
performs a function
beyond any ritual use
or crude attempt
at self-disguise
it is the price
of my survival
forged upon
a mortal alloy
flesh and hair
fitted to a shallow
mold of bone
for posterity

Anemone

It's the deadliest beach in California,
according to our elder daughter,
but I don't see it.
                      We take a picture
sitting on a huge bleached tree trunk
beyond the blind ocean's treacherous reach.

She pleads with me not to go nearer
to the rough surface.
                      Seals, seagulls
and pelicans brave the elemental
menace that her brightly-colored,
weathered toenails indicate.

A crab's disembodied pincer proves
the threat obscurely justified.

I make the upturned roots a throne
and crown my safety with this majestic
jetsam.
        My wife swims in the river
behind us.
             No tsunami claims us,
despite the slapstick warning signs.

We are four refugees, now cautious explorers
who have escaped a hurricane
called cancer.
                Now nothing will ever
be the same, not even on Jenner
Beach.
      Air is misty to the touch
of my shaking hands.
                  A riptide
within my blood rolls on
and carries me
                beyond the sound

and puny fury of my family,
until I glimpse between the breakers
the washed-up, wasted corpse of an enemy.

Retrospective

a morning ramble
in the mountains
punctuated
by the noble dung
of horses
every strenuous step
I thought I'd never
take again
has brought me closer
to finding this
a railroad bridge
a waterfall
a hopscotch of islands
in a wide stream
then around
a corner
a view
of the distance
we've travelled
since we left the car
and scrambled up
this hoof-beaten slope
till our legs ached
and our lungs
swelled up
to shout down
echoes of delight
where tiny regrets
reverberate
and vanish
soundless
a rider and his mount
pause by the water
an incarnation
of such grace
and power
we finally see

we have reached
a place
from which we can
return
to our future

No Calvary

voluntarily
on a cool evening
in my own car
I am returning
to my place of agony

not a Calvary
after all

I feel as if
this were any place
made freshly aware
of possibilities
like summer
and the scent
of magnolia blossoms
and the stillness
of endless air

the Cancer Center
is just a way
to be indoors

neither terminal
nor point
of sharp departure

innocent
of sufferings past
and ignorant
of the fatal future

this

is all
I will ever have
to show why

I survived
our impassioned
encounter

Returning from my Latest Infusion

the piano lessons
have resumed
my daughter remembers
enough to return
from her former recalcitrance
into deft eagerness
the notes climb the stairs
with me as I rally
my limited forces
into awareness
of octaves and keys
while the paces of play
resound with their own
emotional music
andante
allegro
moderato
a fortress of quiet
sings in its frame
untouched for so long
in three-quarter time
she plunks an old harmony
thumping and tingling
like the refreshment
of blood in my veins
after much absence
I have come home

The Forms

In the dirt, wooden forms await
permission to prop up poured concrete.

The raw materials of our future
together, entrenched yet in limbo, hover,
poised above dugouts.
                        A workbench gathers
intentions, like dust, when the wind picks up.

The hired hard labor, sorely wanted here,
is needed elsewhere.
                        Still, the plot lines are clear
and proper to us.
                  We know where we are,
how things will take shape, rearrange the air
around our back porch.
                        We'll impose a staircase,
enclose a shower, feature a waterfall.

No one will care that once our schemes
were just a scar in tormented earth.

The best buttress is death, barely averted.

We can only press on against
that fragile, friable backbone, building
our castles in *terra infirma,*
lumping our lives in with all we acquire.

Morning Glory

a naïve name
conceals a tortuous
climb
the clinging tendrils
hang precarious
clarion blues
from the front corner
of our verandah
untwist their spurts
of fugitive purples
delicate
burgeoning pinks
a budding
persistence
of quivering
heliotropes that
subside as they near
their forbidding
objective
their trumpets catch fire
and flare out
a fragrant
premature judgment
beauty this fragile
means everything
even survival
depends on it
our whole house
leans upon
this plant
and not
the other way round

Brad Buchanan's writings have appeared in more than 200 journals, and he has published three previous book-length collections of poetry: *The Miracle Shirker* (Poet's Corner Press, 2005), *Swimming the Mirror: Poems for My Daughter* (Roan Press, 2008), and *The Scars, Aligned: A Cancer Narrative* (Finishing Line Press, 2019). Now Emeritus Professor of English at Sacramento State University, he has also published two academic books and numerous scholarly articles. His most recent book is a medical memoir entitled *Living with Graft-Versus Host Disease: How I Stopped Fighting Cancer and Started Healing* (Armin Lear Publishing, 2021). He was diagnosed with a rare form of T-cell lymphoma in February 2015, and after chemotherapy and radiation, he underwent a stem cell transplant in early 2016. The transplant, though successful, brought on temporary vision loss and disability, a compromised immune system, and an ongoing illness: acute, then chronic, graft-versus-host disease (GvHD). Late in 2016, he underwent an experimental treatment through a clinical trial for malignant B-cell lymphoma (caused by the Epstein-Barr virus); he is currently in remission.

www.ingramcontent.com/pod-product-compliance
Lightning Source LLC
Chambersburg PA
CBHW030222170426
43194CB00007BA/834